THIS IS

MY LIFE

STORY

THIS IS MY LIFE STORY

A catalogue record for this book is available from the British Library.

First Edition 2020.

First published in Great Britain in 2020 by Carpet Bombing Culture.

An imprint of Pro-actif Communications.

Email books@carpetbombingculture.co.uk

©CarpetBombingCulture
Written by Patrick Potter

ISBN: 978-1-908211-82-8

www.carpetbombingculture.co.uk
www.1millionlifestories.com

TITLE:

....

....

....

THE AUTOBIOGRAPHY OF:

....

Introduction

WELCOME TO
YOUR LIFE STORY

What you are about to do is a very special thing, when you stop to think about it. In the rush of life, we get so lost in the pushing forward, the always moving toward the next thing, that we very rarely reflect. And when we do stop for a second and see some kind of meaning reveal itself in the events and details of our lives – we rarely record that thinking.

So when you put pen to paper, even if you only write a few lines of half thoughts and ideas, you create something utterly unique. You create something that will grow in value with every passing year, a magical thing – a piece of living history.

If you've made it here, you've already thought about writing your story, or at least some of your exploits, for the edification of those to come. And if you answer the questions in this book, picking and choosing whichever question triggers a response, you'll soon find you have made a piece of familial treasure. And all this in a matter of weeks, not years. This is a time capsule of you.

And who knows? Maybe you'll do it again in ten years. Because the story isn't over yet, and every time you tell it, it will grow with you.

A life story is like a river, you never step in the same one twice.

WELCOME

Congratulations, you've chosen to do something adventurous today.

You have decided to do something a little bit special. Today is the day you're going start to write down some of your life story.

Maybe even just a few fragments, half an idea or a few words you remember that someone special used to say. It doesn't matter how much, it doesn't matter what.

Because you're creating something unique.

Reflection is real magic. Reflection is a superpower.

When we're in the thick of it all, living moment to moment (but of course never really in the moment) we always think that life is elsewhere. We think of ourselves the only boring person living on a planet filled with people living lives of heroism and unknown pleasures. We're hard wired to adapt, finding the familiar dull and commonplace, not thinking that our own stories are worth telling. This life? Who on earth would care!?

It's only when we look back that we realise this wasn't true. We were right in the centre of something utterly fragile and unique. Our struggles as epic as any Hercules', our moments as wondrous and bizarre as any tale from the Arabian Nights.

NOTHING IS TRIVIAL

Your life is unique

Unique, even though it is also, of course,
an experience like seven billion others.

That is the weird paradox of being human, we are all utterly the
same and utterly different at every level of the incomprehensibly
enormous tapestry of human lived experience.

You're a thread in that infinite carpet, your lazy Sunday afternoons
an inflection in a shimmering pattern of indescribable beauty.

An interconnectedness never more keenly felt than when crisis
hits, thrown together in our need for each other, a recognition of
the essential nature of our collaboration even while we most need
physical distance. Connected in every sense of the word.

Even though our lives feel so small, they are so interconnected
that every detail echoes through the web of links that bind us. The
epic arises out of the everyday. And looking back is the only time
we ever catch a glimpse of this.

*Your life is one thread
in an infinite carpet*

*The epic arises out of the everyday.
And looking back is the only time
we ever catch a glimpse of this.*

YOU'RE ALREADY
A STORYTELLER

A wise photographer once said, if you want to be a famous photographer, take photographs of everything normal, everything ordinary, all the most mundane details of life – then leave them in a box for twenty years.

To look back is wise, to look back with a pen in your hand, now that really is boxing clever.

Because every time you write from your memory, you realise how much of your memory is wonderful fiction. It is not fictional in the sense of being a lie, but just because subjectivity is like that, perspective is like that, the ego is like that.

The ego weaves a point of view from so many bits of meaningless content, smells, objects, sights, sounds, half perceived the first time around, and then recreated in the alchemist's laboratory of your brain, for whatever purposes your present self demands. Memory is a waking dream and writing it down is like hunting butterflies. You don't need your memories to be complete, definitive or even essentially accurate – you are sketching. Let it be.

Autobiographical writing is the hardest type of fiction, precisely because you experience your life and your memory without the need to boil it down to a single viewpoint or structured narrative, a story that makes sense to others, nor is even interesting to others. Here, we try to make it simple for you by posing a question and giving you a finite space within which to answer it. It's much easier to be interviewed than to do battle with a blank page. Much easier to be given creative space within strict limits.

We put our experience into words constantly,
the trick is not to think about it.

Writing is not memory and reading is not telepathy. The alchemy is in making subjective experience into an object to be shared.

But don't worry about any of that, if you're a seasoned writer of any kind, or if you've avoided writing like the plague ever since you left school, voice is everything in this game, and everyone has a voice. Everyone is a storyteller and every life is a story to tell.

TALKING TO MYSELF

Fix in your mind a picture of who you are writing to.
For many of us, it will be our children, or their children,
or anyone from a world yet to come.

Imagine one day, your imagined or real great grandchildren
fumbling through the contents of dusty old boxes in the attic and
discovering this book. Keep that in mind. A writer always needs to
think about who they are writing to. Not an audience in the plural,
just an audience of one – it's just easier to write to one person as
if you were having an intimate conversation with someone yet to
come, an idealised listener, a young person who actually wants to
listen to their elders!

And they will, you know, ironically, outrageously, they will when
you write it down, because that is the power of publication.
Things you wouldn't be able to tell them face to face, because they
wouldn't care, they'd glaze over or you'd not find the words or
you'd have something else to do. They'll listen to words you have
written before they'll ever remember to give you a call.

Writing is a godsend in this respect. It makes it easier to speak
about yourself, because you become the hero in a story of your
own telling, rather than just, you know, plain old you. And making
yourself into an object helps to put a bit of distance between you
and the subject. You see yourself more clearly when you are a
character in your own book.

So speak softly and carry a big pen. Take some time to get hold of a pen that makes you feel happy. No, really. Pens can spark joy. I mean you can do finger painting if you really want but a beautiful pen can bring you back to the page again and again just for the joy of it.

And work like all the best writers work. Trick yourself into being productive with brute force applications of limited time. Set a clock. Write until the timer is up. This will temporarily kill your inner editor. Your inner fear of stopping writing will trump your inner fear of writing badly every time.

You're not writing anyway, you're just thinking with a pen, or chatting to a book, or doodling with words . . . you get the picture. Because whatever you write, no matter how banal, will be fascinating for it's perspective.

YOU ARE
AN EYEWITNESS

You have lived through a period of history and social change where the past century changed more rapidly than the twenty previous centuries combined.

When they started the mass observation project back in the 1940's they already had some idea that this was a moment, this was a time when things were about to change. And they were right of course. Now the mass-observation diaries are a national treasure.

Imagine what one million copies of this book in the hands of one million people from across the whole world would achieve? What an incredible archive that would be! Even if they were half finished, partial, scrappy and coffee stained things. Perhaps even more so. Because they would be a beautiful, human piece of living history, from a time in which almost all human culture is created and consumed in the vast underground servers of the ineffable cloud.

PAPER IS DEAD
LONG LIVE PAPER!

Digital culture is not everything. And it's full spectrum dominance ensures that any tactile object, created by the living hands of our ancestors will be a trillion times more valuable, because they'll be scarce. And in the oceans of junk data, and all the lost passwords, much of what we share online will be lost. And even if it isn't, the intimacy of writing to that one imaginary great grandchild, is always going to trump the broadcasting tone of social media.

Social media is a place where we pretend to be anything other than exactly what we are.

You, on your own with your favourite pen, in your favourite chair, deep in a flow state of memory and composition, speaking softly with a pen, opening up to a bit of good old fashioned storytelling, that's a voice that'll stand out a million miles from the average post on social media.

So here we are. We need to start light, get comfortable, get the basic facts straight for the audience. Remember, one day this book might be in the hands of someone who doesn't even know your name, let alone remember your face, the sound of your voice, your taste in wallpaper...

MY QUEST

*At some point in our early lives
we realise it.*

We have a purpose.
We need to fulfil a promise that we made,
perhaps to our parents, maybe to ourselves
or even to the world that created us.

Think of all the people involved in the phenomenal task of taking a human infant and making it into an independent actor on the stage of adult life. It's bloody hard work. And we feel that debt. We want to be useful, that's natural, that's being a pack animal, which we are.

So there is the Soul Quest, the thing that we are here to do even though we often can't put it into words, and we feel doubts, such doubts.

But anyway, telling stories about ourselves is ancient, it is as old as language, and it has the power to make meaning. Meaning can be a type of healing.

The story is a psychic technology.

It is the toolkit we use to make the meaning saturated universe we choose to live in. You just have to be open to other stories, as well as your own, and suddenly; the world is an endlessly fascinating place, where there is no room for boredom of any kind.

And this reverie is the closest thing to true empathy we can experience.

*Stories are like fractals, self similar
at every level of magnification.
A book has a beginning, middle and end.
So does a chapter, a paragraph, a beat.*

TELLING STORIES

A whole life contains infinite possible stories, when looked at under an infinite microscope. And when you stand way back, and squint, on a clear day, one single thread emerges as the dominant plot. The building blocks at each level are the same, protagonist, situation, goal, conflict, resolution.

You will find these ingredients as much in a laid back Sunday afternoon as in the major battles of your life. Here, in this book you're being asked to pick the stories that mean most to you, that stayed with you. Because these are likely to be the first one's that come to mind, and the most interesting to your readers.

Sometimes a portrait of a lazy afternoon is exactly the right story to tell. Drama needs light and shade. Even tragedies have comic relief.

The stories you write will not all be obvious in their impact or their meaning. The whole point is not to think about it too much. You'll write what you write. And there is an alchemy in that moment of choice, when your pen hits the page and one story is told while a million others are not...

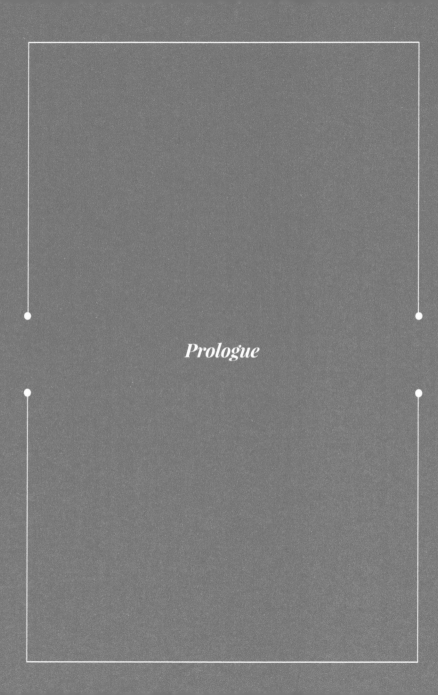

Prologue

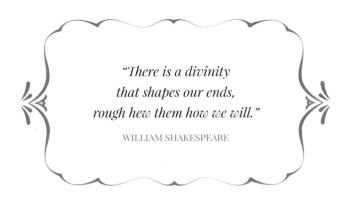

> *"There is a divinity*
> *that shapes our ends,*
> *rough hew them how we will."*
>
> WILLIAM SHAKESPEARE

In other words, no matter how much of a pig's ear we make of our lives, when we look back it always feels like things happened for a reason. You can choose to believe that your life has meaning, and in that choice you make it meaningful.

We are meaning makers. We make meaning out of chaos, and that maybe is the entire point of being human. We make a random universe make sense, even if only to us.

A prologue is a bit of backstory at the beginning of a story. They have fallen out of fashion these days - but hey let's bring it back. Because it's the ideal place to tell a story about your parents, and how they came to make the monumentally excellent decision - to create a tiny baby - you.

Note: Of course not everybody knew their biological parents, and you might feel like you want to write about one parent and not another for whatever reason. Do what works for you, and interpret the questions in any way that makes sense to you. This is your book, your rules.

CHAPTER 1

The Lost World

Childhood is the Lost World. Childhood is Eden.
The gates we leave through are guarded. We can never go back,
except in dreams, and of course stories.

*The doorway to Narnia is just about big enough
for grown ups to pass through.*

Small wonder then that the most important stories of all time,
enormous world sweeping success stories like Harry Potter,
are golden tickets to a holiday in a land called innocence.

Perhaps we should be grateful, we'll never feel fear in the
same way a child does. We'll never know again what it feels like
for an afternoon to last a hundred years, or to be totally at the
mercy of the whims of giants.

Raw, fascinating – possibly even dangerous,
it's an adventure to throw yourself into your own childhood.
Trying to plug yourself in to those endless numbered days can
dredge up all kinds of stuff. But stories have to start somewhere.
And your readers want to know about those early years,
because that's the crucible in which you were formed,
and you are the lead role in this book.

The Little Prince reminds us:

"All grown-ups were once children...
but only few of them remember it."

And the first story of any life, is a love story.
The two people who came together, however briefly,
to make you. And the second story is a violent conflict.
That is to say, a birth story. And that's a story
you've very probably heard many times.

And the third story is 'The Four Hundred Blows',
a childhood story. Usually involving a home,
a cast of idiosyncratic supporting characters,
a school and a hailstorm of minor indignities.
Some scrapes, a few japes and the occasional tragedy.

By the end of this first chapter, the reader will understand
a little better, why you are the way you are, your drives,
your desires and your quest, all of which are rooted
in your first decade...

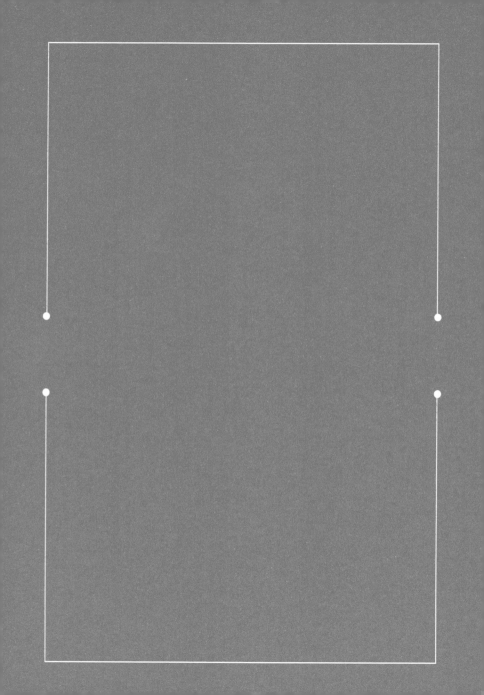

ACT ONE

Childhood

CHAPTER 1

1.1: The Third Act of a Love Story

˅
꙳

My parents met in a place at a time. This is all I know of that story,
it happened something like this...

....

....

....

....

....

....

....

....

....

....

....

....

....

....

1.2: As a Babe

And this is all I know of my first year on Earth.

1.3: My Earliest Memories

These are the first memories I can call my own.
This was the beginning of my autobiographical memory...

....

....

....

....

....

....

....

....

....

....

....

....

....

1.4: My Mother's House Has Many Rooms

I let my mind wander in the rooms of the homes I spent my childhood in. Drifting through those spaces, listening, looking, and this is what I found...

....

....

....

....

....

....

....

....

....

....

....

1.5: My Shining Morning Face

Here is a story from my first school, with as much detail as I can recall. The setting, the cast, the feelings, and why I think they stayed with me.

....

....

....

....

....

....

....

....

....

....

....

....

....

....

1.6: My Family

Here is my opportunity to describe in loving detail,
the familial rituals that made us a family.

1.7: Best Friends Forever

Here I sketch out some fragments of my own stories of my best friends, the sweet and the bitter, the boredom and the hysteria...

....

....

....

....

....

....

....

....

....

....

....

....

....

1.8: A Journey that Changed My Life

Stories are about movement and stories are about change. Here is a story from my childhood, a trip to somewhere new or a repeated journey with a twist, that led to a moment that changed me...

....

....

....

....

....

....

....

....

....

....

....

....

....

1.9: Big School

A portrait of myself coming face to face with one of the great early challenges of my life - moving up to big school, leaving behind the world of unconditional love to enter the world of hard won meritocracy.

1.10: Leaving the Garden

There was a moment when I no longer belonged in the childhood world in which I still found myself, and the siren song of the next world was imminent and powerful, and I knew that I was leaving the garden forever...

....

....

....

....

....

....

....

....

....

....

....

....

....

1.11: Lessons in Life

This is what my childhood taught me...

....

....

....

....

....

....

....

....

....

....

....

....

....

....

CHAPTER 2

The Teenage Years

It starts at different times for different people, but let's say it starts at 13, the official beginning, and ends on that desperate 19th birthday party. This is the second great mind storm of your life. The years when your brain rewires itself almost as fundamentally as it did in the first two years after birth.

You enter a civilised creature, you leave a hormonal monster, re-engineered by primal forces and re-engineered by society as an independent, 'productive' labourer.

This is the infamous adolescence. The first catastrophe.
Nobody has it easy.

Some have it worse than others. Where was it? What was it? What handful of moments can summarise it all for you? Can you cast your mind back to those strange days?

Everything seemed so important. Everything felt like it was happening to you and you alone under some galactic spotlight. You were the first human on earth, and all experience was intense. Almost always intensely something, intensely bored a lot of the time. A series of firsts.

Long past the gloss of innocence, under a new level of adult scrutiny, always making mistakes, the ego emerging, fighting for an individual self - set apart from the family, leaving the parental cocoon, trying to be something more than an ant in an anthill, yet desperate to be normal at the same time.

This was adolescence, strange now that it is all filmed and broadcast, lucky for those who remember when teenagers didn't carry cameras.

The Teenage Years

CHAPTER 2

2.1: Institutionalised

*Here is a portrait of my school life, the hierarchy, the social map,
the pain and the glory, a teacher I loved and a teacher I didn't get on with,
the sights, sounds and smells...*

....

....

....

....

....

....

....

....

....

....

....

....

....

....

2.2: Sighing Like a Furnace

And they called it puppy love. This is the story of early experiences, pricking my teenaged fingers on the thorns of love. The days I began to realise that maybe boys or girls were not urgh after all...

....

....

....

....

....

....

....

....

....

....

....

....

....

....

2.3: My Teenage Obsessions

Was it a hobby or a band? A celebrity or a religion?
Was it a sport or an art? When I was a teenager I was obsessed with...

....

....

....

....

....

....

....

....

....

....

....

....

....

2.4: My Subculture

And one day I felt like I had finally found my lost tribe, my people and I realised that I was amongst others who felt the same and I would be until the day I died...

....

....

....

....

....

....

....

....

....

....

....

....

2.5: Sanctuary

The bedroom is the chrysalis of the teenager.
This is a story about a bedroom, mine or a friend's, a place of sanctuary...

2.6: Friends and Enemies

A story about falling out, perhaps for a while, perhaps forever.
Adolescence is when our conflicts suddenly develop consequences.
Those first cuts were deep...

....

....

....

....

....

....

....

....

....

....

....

....

....

2.7: Don't know much about Biology

At the most difficult time of my human life, the adults somehow decided it was a brilliant idea to throw dozens of extremely high stakes academic exams at me. This is the story of how I dealt with all that...

....

....

....

....

....

....

....

....

....

....

....

....

....

....

2.8: Sex, Drugs and Rock and Roll

Either you discovered them or you refused them,
but there was no escaping them.

2.9: A question of doubt

Moments of self loathing and doubt go hand in hand with being a teenager. This is a story about when I felt an outcast.

CHAPTER 3

Very Heaven

The idea of youth is the defining principle of western culture,
the most powerful invention of the Twentieth Century and
supposedly, the peak, the prime, the halcyon moment
of all of our blessed lives. But was it all it cracked up to be?
Was it wasted on the young? Because it's easy to forget
how tough it was.

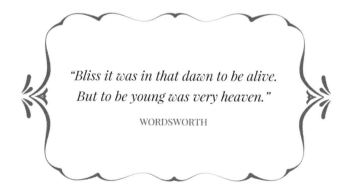

*"Bliss it was in that dawn to be alive.
But to be young was very heaven."*

WORDSWORTH

Under the enormous pressure of being supposed to be having 'The Time of Our Lives' and yet so deprived of any access to resources with which to achieve this, without experience, without capital, without saleable skills, fumbling and stumbling through a series of long hard years trying to pay our dues, earn our stripes, get skin in the game, all of which sound painful, because they were.

And somewhere in all of that, there were those moments, those blissful moments of being young and having all the doors open and all the possibilities alive and dancing in our minds, and the camaraderie, the sharing of experience with our friends, friendships like you never have in later life, relationships, wild nights and lazy days. Friends as family.

And what handful of these moments will you choose to recall here, in the book of your life?

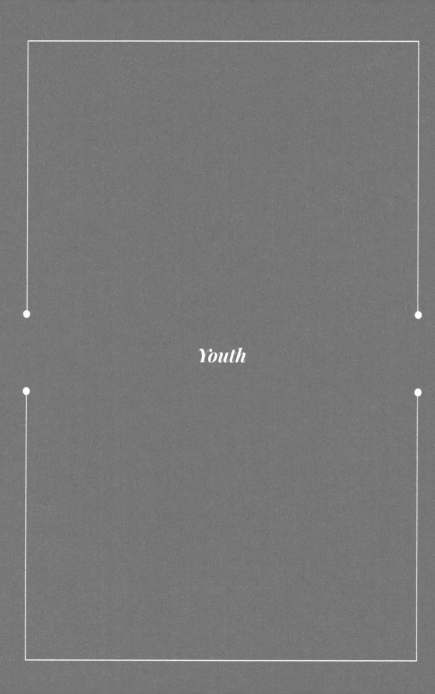

Youth

CHAPTER 3

3.1: The Best Times of My Teenage Years

A montage...

....

....

....

....

....

....

....

....

....

....

....

....

....

....

3.2: Consequences

The craziest thing I ever did, and am now willing to confess on paper, whether I got caught at the time or not...

3.3: A time and a place that I have Known and Loved

I remember a time and place where we were all young, gifted and broke, and we were very new at learning how to live without adult assistance...

3.4: When I Discovered I was Not Immortal

My Icarian moment, a time I flew too close to the sun...

3.5: My Most Epic Failure

This was my first taste of adult level failure...

....

....

....

....

....

....

....

....

....

....

....

....

....

3.6: A Portrait of Me

What am I like? How do I dress? How do I talk?
A self-portrait in words...

3.7: My People

*The most important group of friends in my younger years,
the people who form a part of who I still am now, the people who are still
voices in my head, were...*

....

....

....

....

....

....

....

....

....

....

....

....

....

3.8: My Most Epic Adventure

A journey, a victory, an experience. Something daring.
Something risked. Something to remember forever...

3.9: Lessons in Life

What youth taught me...

CHAPTER 4

Only Love Can Break Your Heart

Shakespeare's lover was a sighing teenager, but love stories can strike at any time, any stage of life. Don't feel constrained to writing only about young love here. You want people to read this? You gotta have a love story, or three...

Romance is the most popular genre of fiction of all time.

The french courtiers who invented the novel, wrote Romances. Romance is everything, because it is EVERYTHING. All life comes from it. The very survival of our species depends on it. The next generation is built upon foundations made of sighs.

You gotta have Romance - and here you need to make a decision, about how much detail you want to share. Because of course, you can fade to black at a classy moment. Play it again Sam.

Nothing beats a good love story. And yours have the benefit of being real, steeped in the situational reality of a particular moment in time, and they also have the benefit of being the creation stories of the next generation, family in whatever sense of the word is relevant to you, who will read your love stories like young acolytes poring over the book of Genesis.

Love stories are powerful, they get retold again and again, defining the reality of a relationship, forming it's foundations. And stories of heartbreak too, are among the most universal because that pain is universal and all people seek to learn from the mistakes of others, or see patterns in the mistakes of their ancestors, shedding light on their own.

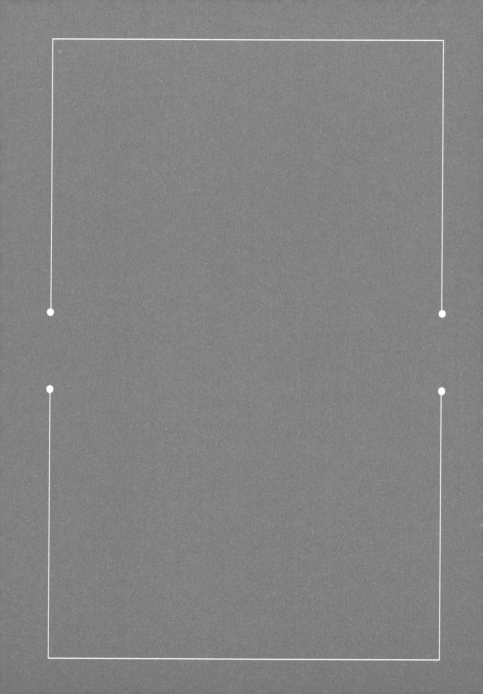

ACT TWO

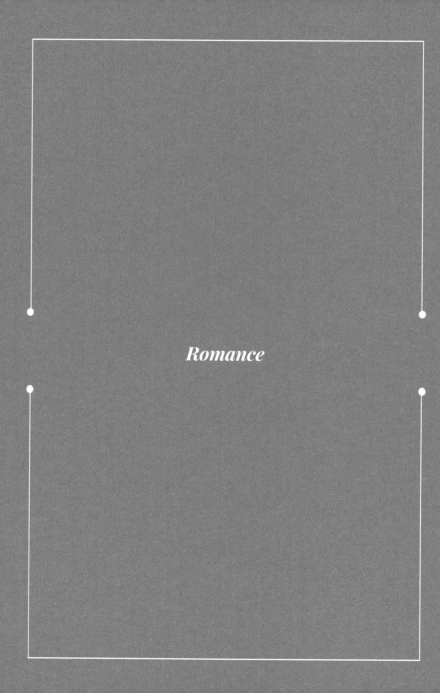

Romance

CHAPTER 4

4.1: The First

I shall attempt here to tell the story of that first rollercoaster of emotions that was falling in love, or perhaps something like love, and then falling out of it...

4.2: The Jack of Hearts

A story of a romantic escapade worthy of a scandal.
Something to tickle the grandkids. A time you were a little bit careless
about the rules of engagement.

4.3: Only Love Can Break Your Heart

A heartbreak so profound that it fundamentally changed me...

4.4: Life is not a Movie

The most unconventional experience of romance I ever had, the biggest shock, the most tragicomic error in love...

....

....

....

....

....

....

....

....

....

....

....

....

....

....

4.5: A Romantic Proposal

This is how that romantic commitment took place.

....

....

....

....

....

....

....

....

....

....

....

....

....

4.6: The Most Romantic Journey

This is the story of the most romantic trip, the most romantic place, the most romantic experience I ever had.

4.7: The One - The Fall

The single most important love story of my life.
The one that had the greatest impact on me. This is how we met,
and everything that followed...

....

....

....

....

....

....

....

....

....

....

....

....

....

4.8: The One - Back to Back Against the World

Love is not staring into each other's eyes, it's staring in the same direction.
A portrait of the partnership we became. Our finest hours. Our struggles.
The story of our relationship and the fruits it bore.

....

....

....

....

....

....

....

....

....

....

....

....

....

....

4.9: The One - Falling in Love Again (Or not)

A time we fell in love with each other again. Or an ending perhaps, because even the greatest loves can fall apart...

....

....

....

....

....

....

....

....

....

....

....

....

....

4.10: Baby I Love You

There is another kind of romance, with fewer songs written, because people are too tired to write songs when they're in love with a baby. This is a story of falling in love with a child...

....

....

....

....

....

....

....

....

....

....

....

....

....

....

4.11: Lessons in Life

What relationships have taught me...

CHAPTER 5

My Mission on Earth

The best stories are about characters who want something really bad. At some point in our life, we all feel the call of the soul quest, even though we find it very hard to figure out just what our purpose is exactly – we know we long for something, and we begin to struggle to get towards it.

They say nobody tells you that the second great love story of your life is your career. That is if you're lucky enough to have a career. But somehow we do seem to end up with one, no matter how much it feels like we are pinballs in a gigantic pinball machine.

Some time in our early lives we are tossed into the wilderness by more or less enthusiastic parents and carers, and we must endure that wilderness time, a few years perhaps or maybe twenty, when work is a horrendous march through a hostile territory.

But one day, something changes, people seem to actually listen to you, mainly because you're older, but also perhaps because you've accidentally become good at something, or many things.

The story of work is seldom told, it doesn't generally make Saturday night commercial cinema, unless you're a musician or a sports star, but it is one of the most fascinating stories we can tell.

How will you tell yours?

When was it that you realised what your calling, your mission was?

Career

CHAPTER 5

5.1: My Soul Quest

This is the story of how I realised what my vocation was...

....

....

....

....

....

....

....

....

....

....

....

....

....

5.2: Workmates

Some of the tightest friendships we have are forged in the heat of shared adversity, in those awful jobs we have toiled at. Here is a sketch of some that shared the journey...

5.3: The Wilderness Years

A clutch of anecdotes from the worst jobs I ever had...

....

....

....

....

....

....

....

....

....

....

....

....

....

5.4: Customers, Bosses and other Animals

An anecdote about serving the most irrational creatures on Earth, human beings.

5.5: A Skill I Earned

Something I got really good at, and how it happened.

5.6: The Greatest Job I Ever Had

Paid or unpaid, employed or self-employed, my best endeavour was...

5.7: The Work I Want to be Remembered For

That time it all came together, and I got to do something that mattered for people who deserved it...

....

....

....

....

....

....

....

....

....

....

....

....

....

....

5.8: The Story of My Career (Without Spin)

It's unusually freeing to be able to tell the story of my working life without having to make it all sound like it was planned...

....

....

....

....

....

....

....

....

....

....

....

....

....

CHAPTER 6

My Struggle

No good story comes without conflict.

Picking out the pivotal battles of your life will bring this book kicking and screaming out of the category of staid memoir and into the category of gripping biopic.

You decide how much of your trauma you want to share, and need to share, and are certain your readers will be ready for you to share. Here we try to tease out the major defining antagonisms in your life, be they human enemies or social forces, not to mention your inner demons. Of course they are reflections of one another.

The best stories combine external and internal conflict, because that's how life tends to work, and the best stories teach us how to cope with the pain of being alive.

So if your conflicts are subtle, no matter, if they were less subtle, all good too. Map them closely with your internal shifts, the battles you fought inside and you'll find you have a story they'll want to option for a TV series.

Crisis & Conflict

CHAPTER 6

6.1: The Theme

Each life has many conflicts, but great stories have one major theme. This is the true thematic conflict of my life, the one I played out many times in many ways...

6.2: The War of Love

A story of a conflict or a skirmish in the war of love.

6.3: Class War

A time I experienced a clash of social class.

....

....

....

....

....

....

....

....

....

....

....

....

....

....

6.4: It's Just Business

The most painful financial struggle I experienced,
and how it changed me.

....

....

....

....

....

....

....

....

....

....

....

....

....

....

6.5: Neighbours

A story of the worst kind of politics, micropolitics...

6.6: A Fight

❧

A story of real physical or emotional struggle.

6.7: The Abyss

*The lowest point of my entire life, the point at which I thought
I would fail in every way, all hope lost.*

....

....

....

....

....

....

....

....

....

....

....

....

....

6.8: Rebirth

A time I discovered a strength I never knew that I had.

CHAPTER 7

Peaking

Why is being middle aged the punchline of every joke?

This time of life, so often lampooned and derided, so often laughed at for the crime of no longer being YOUNG and yet for many the absolute and genuine prime of life, young enough to enjoy being at the height of your powers, old enough to be effective and focussed, terrifyingly productive, capable of making things happen that young people can only talk about.

But also it is a time of conflict, a time of being worried about your elders and your children, or nephews, nieces, or youth in general. Tormented by ambition, loss, ageing bodies and that sense of time...running...out...

You're under the whip, struggling with a wildly varying and often conflicting set of roles and responsibilities. Wearing too many hats. Spinning too many plates, not waving but drowning.

And somehow, in the midst of all this, maybe winning some of the most important victories of your life, while trying to remember on occasion, to be in the moment (whatever that is)

It thunders by. Hold back that river!

Can you catch a moment and put it in a jar?

The Middle Years

CHAPTER 7

7.1: A Shock

A rare moment of absolutely unexpected adversity,
a totally shocking turnaround, a surprise reversal of fortunes...

....

....

....

....

....

....

....

....

....

....

....

....

....

....

....

7.2: My Addictions

We all get addicted to something. And here is my confession...

....

....

....

....

....

....

....

....

....

....

....

....

....

7.3: A Healing

*We spend most of our adult life recovering from the trauma
of being young, here is a moment I found some of that healing...*

7.4: A Lighter Moment

Here is a funny story that even now makes me smile.

7.5: A Turning Point

When I look back, so many strands of the storyline of my life
can be traced back to that one pivotal moment...

....

....

....

....

....

....

....

....

....

....

....

....

....

7.6: A Victory

Here is a story about a battle I won in my middle years.

7.7: Where I Was When...

A list of historical turning points, and where I was and what I was doing when they happened, and reflections on how they changed the way I saw the world...

....

....

....

....

....

....

....

....

....

....

....

....

....

....

7.8: A Mentor

This is a sketch of a mentor I had, the relationship between us and the way that it changed me.

....

....

....

....

....

....

....

....

....

....

....

....

....

7.9: A Team

This is a portrait of a team or a partnership I was a part of,
that meant a lot to me, that became a part of me,
and the things we achieved together.

7.10: A Conversation between...

Myself at twenty and myself at fifty.
Here is what they might have said to each other...

....

....

....

....

....

....

....

....

....

....

....

....

....

7.11: An Adversary

*Here is a story about an enemy I faced in my middle years,
whether a person, a force or an inner demon.*

....

....

....

....

....

....

....

....

....

....

....

....

....

....

7.12: A Defeat

Here is a story about a battle I lost in my middle years..

7.13: Children

This is how children came into my life,
this is how it impacted on me and changed me.

....

....

....

....

....

....

....

....

....

....

....

....

....

....

7.14: Lessons in Life

This is what my middle years taught me.

....

....

....

....

....

....

....

....

....

....

....

....

....

....

CHAPTER 8

The Meaning of My Life: Telling Stories

Crescendo.

All stories require a climax. The big finale. The showdown.

What is the most important struggle of your life? If you can answer this question, you can direct the movie.

You can identify the moment when your decisive victories, or decisive defeats played out, all with the benefit of hindsight.

If this were a screenplay for the movie of your life, you'd fudge the details to fit the structure, make sure the final showdown was crystal clear, in reality it's often more subtle than that.

But you'll know what you want to say.

We all know our essential conflict. It's the demons that we have to slay again and again. because we don't live out our essential story once, we repeat it again and again, having to win it or lose it over and over again. Because life, like stories, is fractal-like in it's self-similarity. As above, so below.

We come up against the man or woman in the mirror
again and again.

ACT THREE

My Life as a Story

CHAPTER 8

8.1: The Package

This is the premise of the story of my life, the whole story.

The title of the Movie of my life:

....

....

....

The Opening Scene of the Movie:

....

....

....

....

....

....

....

....

The music playing as the titles appear:

....

....

The closing scene:

....

....

....

....

....

....

....

....

....

....

....

....

....

....

The music playing over the closing credits:

....

....

8.2: The Theme

Here I state the argument of the theme. Love conquers all when... / Good conquers evil when... / Justice prevails when... / Family overcomes when... / A cynic learns to trust when... or something similar.

....

....

....

....

....

....

....

....

....

....

....

....

....

8.3: All the World's a Stage

Act 1 states the theme. Act 2 & 3 debate that theme. Act 4 is synthesis.
Each one ends with a catastrophe that changes everything.

Act 1:
....

....

....

Act 2:
....

....

....

Act 3:
....

....

....

Act 4:
....

....

....

8.4: The Call to Adventure

All the times I felt the call to adventure, and found innumerable reasons to refuse them until the time I finally realised how obvious it was what I should have been doing all along...

....

....

....

....

....

....

....

....

....

....

....

....

....

8.5: Trials and Ordeals

All the times the universe tested my resolve,
and all the while I didn't realise it was forging me into something new...

....

....

....

....

....

....

....

....

....

....

....

....

....

....

8.6: The Abyss

⸱⸱⸱

The mirror moment, the lowest point. The point at which the hero finally commits to taking arms against a sea of troubles...

....

....

....

....

....

....

....

....

....

....

....

....

....

....

....

8.7: Transformation

The final battle climaxes at the point the hero finally realises the truth of the story's theme and uses it to slay the demons both inner and outer, once and for all, transforming not only themselves, but the world.

8.8: Atonement

*Once transformed the hero has the opportunity to set right
all the damage they caused in their deluded original state...*

8.8: The Hero's Return

The hero comes back to the ordinary world bearing a gift, their hard won new understanding of the world, and there is much rejoicing...

CHAPTER 9

The Wisdom Years

*Life changes a gear, you ease out of middle age
and find yourself in a new territory.*

Now perhaps you have landed in a role of respected authority,
but this is a world where stories do not simply end when the
young lovers get married, nor do they end when the peak
moment of your career hits.

And the peak moment of your career (second, third or fiftieth)
and the greatest love story of your life may be happening now,
may still be yet to come...

Stop the press. We continue to live stories, and this may shock the young to discover, but we feel them with just the same intensity as we always did, we win and lose just like we always did, sometimes the stakes are higher, sometimes lower, but the wisdom years are not without conflict.

The battle with entropy, the battle with a society that sidelines it's elders and the struggle to give the next generation a hand up in the ancient war of life, these are the struggles of the wisdom years.

Life As An Elder

CHAPTER 9

9.1: My birthday, a ceremony, an anniversary.

A sketch of an evening, the people and the place.

....

....

....

....

....

....

....

....

....

....

....

....

....

9.2: Later Love

A love story where the lovers are not sighing adolescents composing sonnets about eyebrows.

....

....

....

....

....

....

....

....

....

....

....

....

....

9.3: Mentor

A relationship with a younger person where I played a mentor role.

9.4: A List of Firsts

*All the things I did or achieved for the first time
in my later years.*

....

....

....

....

....

....

....

....

....

....

....

....

....

....

9.5: My Magnum Opus

The greatest piece of work I did (so far) in my later years.

9.6: A Story of Loss

A story of a difficult loss.

....

....

....

....

....

....

....

....

....

....

....

....

....

....

9.7: Old Friends

A story about a good time with an old friend or group of friends.

9.8: The Ravages of Time

A story about health, or the lack of it,
and how I learned to cope with the ravages of time.

9.9: Old Enough to Know Better

A story about being a little wild
when I was really supposed to be being incredibly wise.

9.10: Je ne Regrette Rien

A list of regrets.

....

....

....

....

....

....

....

....

....

....

....

....

9.11: The Best Things About Being Old

Or a story of all the things I do not miss about being younger...

CHAPTER 10

Not Over Yet

And here is a chapter for talking about hopes and dreams.
Because it is not over yet.

And here at the moment that you have made the brave decision
to record your life, you are at yet another turning point. It's a
moment to think about what you want for the future and record
it for posterity, to remind people that it ain't over till the fat lady
sings and you still have time to make a few stories worth telling.

It's time now, to play the role of the wise owl, it is what they
need from you after all, and you can finally say all the things
that they are not allowed to say, truth teller, sage. elder.

Tell 'em what you learned...

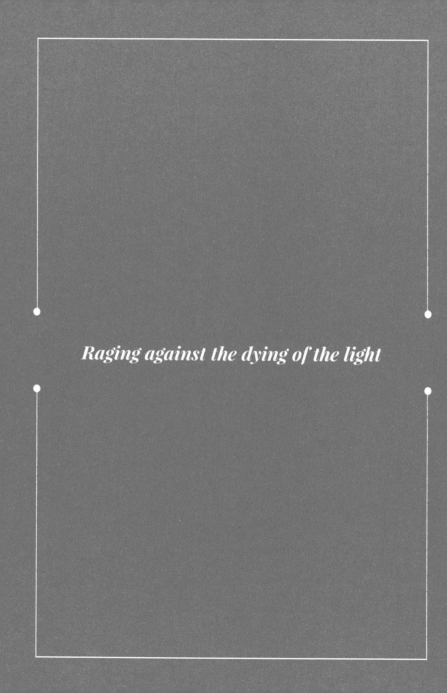

Raging against the dying of the light

CHAPTER 10

10.1: What I Learned

✦

I've been around the Karmic wheel so many times I'm a bit dizzy.
Here is what the Lady Fortuna has taught me...

10.2: I Stand Witness

This is how the world changed in my lifetime.
These are the major turning points I witnessed.

10.3: The Next Century

It's always dangerous to make predictions,
but it's a lot of fun to read them in the future!

10.4: My Legacy

This is what I leave the world.

10.5: A Child I Used to Know

This is everything I would say to myself at the age of seven.

....

....

....

....

....

....

....

....

....

....

....

....

....

....

10.6: Thank You Everything

A letter of thanks to everything and everyone I feel grateful to for having been a part of my life.

....

....

....

....

....

....

....

....

....

....

....

....

....

....

10.7: The Most Fun I Have Had Recently

This is the most fun I have had in the last twelve months...

10.8: The Next Adventure

This is an adventure that I am preparing to embark upon,
a new thing to learn, a new place to go, a new skill or new creation...

10.9: DIY Obituary

I can't promise this is all true,
but here is the obituary you'll need to forward to the Times...

....

....

....

....

....

....

....

....

....

....

....

....

....

....

10.10: My Last Goodbye

This is how I imagine my funeral. These are the songs I want you to play.
These are the inappropriate jokes I want you to tell...

....

....

....

....

....

....

....

....

....

....

....

....

....

MY LIFE IN 100 QUESTIONS

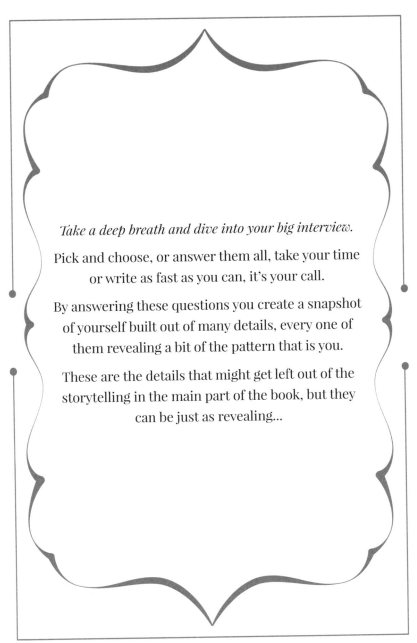

Take a deep breath and dive into your big interview.

Pick and choose, or answer them all, take your time or write as fast as you can, it's your call.

By answering these questions you create a snapshot of yourself built out of many details, every one of them revealing a bit of the pattern that is you.

These are the details that might get left out of the storytelling in the main part of the book, but they can be just as revealing...

I was born in

The most precious thing in my life

My earliest memory

A List of all the Places I lived

Happiness is

A list of all my closest Friends

People tell me I look like

My soulmate

My favourite pet

What I order in a restaurant

The teacher who had the biggest impact on me

Growing up I wanted to be a

The one memory that I visualize most frequently is

The thing I miss most from my past

My favourite word

My sport

My game

My favourite movie

My favourite actor

My favourite book

The song that reminds me of my childhood

The TV show I love to watch

My favourite holiday destination

My favourite season

The turning point in my life

The artist I admire

My favourite drink

My favourite food

My happy place

My release

My guilty pleasure

My languages

The thing that keeps me awake at night

The song that I return to

A list of all the countries I have visited

A list of all my jobs

The person I feel most protective over

A list of my interests

A list of things that annoy me

The most exciting thing in my life

The most painful thing in my life

The most beautiful thing in my life

The thing about me almost nobody knows

The age that I became an adult

The period of history I wish I'd been born in

If I could spend one day with anyone living or dead, it would be

My signature dish

Last time I cried

Last time I laughed

The book I always wanted to read

The actor who would play me in a movie of my life

My favourite school subject

A club or society that I was part of

Things that people typically get me for gifts

If I woke up tomorrow with no fear, the first thing I would do is

The lie that I tell myself the most

A bridge that I would like to burn

The biggest miracle in my life

The job I think I would have been good at

The one thing that I know now that I wish that I had known then

When I was a child I . . . .

The bitterest pill I ever had to swallow

My closest brush with death was

The time I was blind to the real truth

A feeling I have which is inexpressible to others

My self worth comes from

The person from history I admire the most

The one thing that I will never give up on

The one thing that I'm holding on to

The fear that drives me

The goal that motivated me

The person who taught me the most

The questions in my life that have remained unanswered

When I think of beauty I think of

When I think of pain I think of

The main 'do's that I have learned in life

The main 'don't's that I have learned in life

If I could live my life all over again, knowing what I know now,
these are the things that I would change

The doors that I walked through

The doors I chose not to open

The forks in the road I took

When I need inspiration I think of

When I close my eyes I see

When I think about unconditional love I think of

My guardian angel(s)

Influencers and motivators

My lucky talisman

The small things that I value

If I had three wishes

My proudest achievement

Something wrong in the world that I think needs fixing

The one thing that I wanted to learn but never did

I want you to know this about my parents

'My World' consisted of this geographical area

The cause I'm dedicated to

The place that I still call home

The greatest love of my life

A little thing that gave me a lot of joy

The best piece of advice I've been given

The best piece of advice I could give

THIS IS MY LIFE STORY: The Things I've Learned

*The lessons, the wisdom, the knowledge, the insight
and the rules to follow, bend or break.*

....

....

....

....

....

....

....

....

....

....

....

....

....

Y TREE

#1MILLIONLIFESTORIES

Our mission is to capture and preserve one million, hand
written, individual life stories from around the world.
Every time somebody completes a copy of 'This Is My Life
Story' simply post I've written my life story! With the
hashtag #1millionlifestories on any social media.

Imagine a world in which millions of life stories are left
behind, each one a shining fragment of a real life,
written in their own hand. Found, for centuries to come,
in boxes in dusty attics, on grandparents' bookshelves,
or even further afield, perhaps left in strange places
for others to find.

#1millionlifestories is a campaign for a new kind of social
history, something you can touch and utterly unique.
Something real in a world of zeros and ones. Handwritten
life stories from every corner of the world.

An incredible record of ordinary people living through
extraordinary times. Like the mass observation project of
the mid-twentieth century, this will be an epic piece of
social history, but told on a human scale. Not the stories of
the powerful, but the stories of the rest of us.

Every voice is unique, every perspective worth sharing.

"I've written my life story!" #1millionlifestories

www.1millionlifestories.com